CW00517782

BUSINESS OUTSOURCING

Table of Contents

Introduction

Companies might consider business outsourcing for many different reasons. Outsourcing might be considered for many different business segments.

Business outsourcing is when a company hires an outside source to complete work or a project which would normally be done by the staff.

A company might consider outsourcing for saving money by cutting down on costs or they might not have the employee resources to complete a particular project.

Outsourcing gives a company the opportunity to complete a needed project performed by people who are not their employees. This means they don't have to pay a salary or provide benefits to the people also.

When business outsourcing occurs, the company will usually enter into an agreement with the outsourcing company which is usually a contract.

The contract will usually include the terms of the agreement like steps throughout the project, time the project will take, people involved, cost, and required resources from the client. There are many different types of outsourcing.

The most common segments of a business that hires outsourcing companies for assistance include accounting services to help with payroll, inventory, and financial issues.

The biggest field of outsourcing today for companies is in the Information Technology field. This is because companies will upgrade their phones, computers, need cabling installed, troubleshooting, and more.

Companies also outsource people for customer service positions, call centers, and telemarketing.

Outsourcing is a solution for a business to save money and complete projects and tasks in the workforce without having full-time employees do the work. Outsourcing is becoming more and more popular across the world every day.

Reasons You Might Consider Business Outsourcing

There are many reasons you might consider outsourcing for your company. Many of those reasons might include resources, cost, or staff.

If you are a growing company, you might have many projects you need to complete for your expansion. If you are upgrading systems, you might have projects you need to complete.

You might not have a staff that knows how to complete the project, or your staff may not have enough people to complete the project in the time frame you would like it to be done.

Outsourcing is an excellent idea when you face issues like this. A company can come into your business and complete the project on your required deadline.

Another reason you might consider outsourcing is to save money. You might currently have full-time employees in positions that only require them to be around for certain times of the year.

It is cheaper to eliminate the full-time employee position and bring in the outsourcing company only when you need them to work.

When you bring in an outsourcing company to complete a project rather than hire a full-time employee you are saving on the yearly salary and the benefits you would have to offer that employee.

In most cases, it is usually cheaper to hire an individual or team of people on a temporary basis then it is to use your own staff. There are many reasons you might consider outsourcing.

You might have a full-time employee you need for one specific thing but often has a lot of downtimes and you have to find work for them to do to keep them busy.

There is no reason to pay a full-time employee if you can hire someone for the duration you need them.

Chapter 1: Finding Ways to Outsource

Are you considering outsourcing but have no idea where to start?

In almost every industry there is the opportunity to outsource at least a few of the common tasks performed in the industry.

In some industries, there may the possibility of outsourcing the majority of the common tasks while in other industries there may only be the opportunity to outsource one or two of the common tasks.

In either case, outsourcing can result in a lightened workload as well as an increase in profit.

Evaluate Daily Activities

The first step in finding ways to outsource is to take a really close look at the daily activities you perform when tending to your business. Make a list of each of these activities and note any related activities that are typically performed in conjunction with each other. Making this note is important because activities that are typically performed together should either be outsourced together or remain as in-house activities together to maintain the highest level of efficiency.

Once you have compiled this list of activities, carefully consider which activities can easily be performed by another person and which activities require your personal attention. This will give you a good idea of which activities you could outsource, and which activities would not be good opportunities for outsourcing.

Finally, review your list of activities and note how long it takes you to perform each of the activities you could outsource. This information will be helpful later if you decide to search for a candidate to complete these tasks.

Prioritize Daily Activities

After you have carefully examined your daily activities, it is time to prioritize these activities. Create a comprehensive list of all of your daily activities in their order of importance. This list includes both the activities requiring your personal attention and the activities which can be outsourced.

When you make your decision to start outsourcing some of your daily tasks, start with the highest priority on the list which you believe can be outsourced. Attempt to outsource this task as a test to determine whether or not outsourcing will work for you.

If you decide you are comfortable with outsourcing and that it is working for your business, you can continue down the prioritized list attempting to find those capable of handling your daily activities.

Consider Administrative Tasks

We have already discussed the importance of evaluating your own daily tasks in the process of finding ways to outsource but it is also important to consider tasks completed by your staff members. Administrative tasks are often tasking that can be outsourced so examining these tasks will give you a good idea if you can increase the efficiency of your administrative assistance by outsourcing some of their responsibilities.

Activities such as data entry, transcription and other activities often handled by personal assistance are all example of activities which can easily be outsourced. Additionally, there is a lot of qualified candidates available to fulfill these tasks.

The industry of virtual personal assistants has become a booming industry with many savvy entrepreneurs offering their skills in these areas as a consultant.

Develop a Plan for Managing Outsourced Activities

Before starting to outsource daily activities, you should develop a plan for managing all of your outsourced activities.

This plan should include the following:

- Method for selecting candidates to handle outsourced work.
- Method for overseeing the work performed by independent contractors.
- Method for evaluating the work performed by independent contractors.

Guide To Outsourcing

Those who are considering outsourcing portions of work for the first time may be feeling overwhelmed and hesitant about the concept of relying on someone outside the company to complete work-related tasks.

Wither discomfort with deciding whether or not to outsource work stems largely from ignorance about the process of outsourcing. This chapter will serve as a guide to those who are considering outsourcing for the first time and will provide information on how to select qualified candidates, establish project requirements, and enforce a deadline for project completion.

Select Qualified Candidates Carefully

One way to greatly simplify the process of outsourcing is to give special consideration to selecting a qualified candidate to complete the outsourced tasks. This is important because outsourcing the project to an individual who is qualified to complete the tasks and motivated to do a good job will make the outsourcing endeavor more likely to be successful.

To find the right candidate for the job, place advertisements outlining the project requirements and preferences, and carefully review each application that is submitted. Immediately disregard applicants who are not qualified for the position.

Then review the applications of qualified candidates carefully and select a small group of the most promising candidates. Next interview each of these candidates and verify their references and past work experiences to learn more about these candidates and their abilities and work ethics.

After interviewing these candidates, it is time to make a decision regarding hiring one of the final candidates. Do not be discouraged if none of the final candidates seemed right for the job because you are under no obligation to hire any of them.

You can continue your search for a qualified candidate by placing your job advertisement again and soliciting new responses.

Establish Definite Requirements

When outsourcing a project or tasks, it is important to clearly define the project requirements. This is critical because it is important for the contractor to fully understand the tasks which are being outsourced to ensure he is fulfilling all of the requirements and satisfactorily complete the task.

Failure to establish definite project requirements and goals can lead to a lot of problems when outsourcing a project. The contractor may feel as though he has completed the project as it was outlined but the employer may disagree. When this happens there can be harmful delays until the issues can be resolved amicably. In the case that this is not possible it might be necessary to employ the assistance of a mediator to evaluate the contract documents and the work produced to determine if the contract terms were met.

Establish a Firm Deadline

Another important element of outsourcing is establishing a firm deadline for the project. This is important to avoid misunderstandings and to prevent late submissions of work.

Setting milestone goals is also important because it gives the employer the ability to evaluate the progress of the contractor during different stages of the project and to ensure it is proceeding according to schedule.

Ideally, the deadline should be established before the candidate is chosen. This is important because this enables the employer to verify that the contractor is available for the duration of the project.

The schedule should be discussed early in the process of selecting a candidate to avoid selecting an ideal candidate only to find out he is unavailable when his services are required.

Chapter 2: Dangers of Business Outsourcing

Business outsourcing is becoming more and more popular each day.

However, you need to be careful when you do decide to hire an outside company for your project.

Some of the problems that may occur are turnover, knowledge, and attitude problems. These can be difficult to handle.

When you hire a business outsourcing company to provide your staff on a temporary basis problems often occur with turnover rates.

Outsourcing companies have a higher turnover rate than most companies and you need to be prepared if you tend
 to go through employees quickly.

When turnover occurs, you have to continue to train them. If you need to pull an employee from their current workload to train a new employee, then this can create a problem with that employee getting behind.

Turnover can also cause problems with the knowledge of the company. When you have to retrain employees about policies and procedures, it might take some time for a new employee to get the hang of things.

Most employers believe it takes approximately two weeks for a new employee to get settled in. However, your customer service may take a hit and you might have customers complaining about your service.

Another thing you need to think about outsourcing is that the employee is not working for you. Many temporary employees want a full-time job with the company they are working for because they need the benefits.

However, when an employee is not really working for you then they don't take on the mission and the vision of the company and believe in instilling it.

Often times, you might see outsourced employees not care about the company as they should. You should ensure all outsourced employees will hold true to the company although they are not really your employee.

Business Outsourcing for Risk Management

When you hire a business outsourcing company for your risk management needs, you need to spell out the context for your risk management process.

The steps should include identification, planning, mapping, defining, developing, and mitigation.

A business outsourcing group is your best option for risk management issues. This is because if something happens you can put the blame on someone else and it is not all on you.

The first step the company will cover is identifying the risks that may occur to the company or the domain of interest.

You will need to establish a plan with the company for the remainder of the process for your risk management.

When you are working with a business outsourcing company, they will map out the social scope of managing risk, the stakeholder's objectives and identity, and the basis risks are evaluated.

They will also determine if any constraints might slow down your project for establishing a good risk management process.

You will then need to establish a framework that will explain an agenda for all activities you need to complete to meet your goals. This will be a process of setting certain timelines for the completion of certain projects.

Once you have worked with your business outsourcing group with these steps you will then need to develop an analysis plan to verify your risk management solution is successful. You will need to mitigate also using the resources available to you.

A business outsourcing company will help you with all of your needs when you need to establish a solid risk management plan for your business.

Communications Problems With Business Outsourcing

If you are looking to save money and thinking about using a business outsourcing company for your telemarketing or your technical support needs, you must consider the communication issues that might arise with outsourcing.

Many times, when people call a customer service or call center for assistance with their account information for a company they complain because there is a language barrier and it is hard to understand what the people are saying.

If you are considering hiring a company for your outsourcing needs, you should ensure that the customer service representative's first spoken language is of the customers who will be calling.

If it is not, it should be guaranteed to you that the representatives will be able to speak your language well enough to understand them.

One way to guarantee the language barrier will not exist with the customer service representatives from the outsourcing company you are hiring is for you and other team members to make phone calls to the representatives who will be representing you.

This way, you and your team members can speak to the individuals and verify if their spoken language is good enough for your customers.

Most communications problems with call centers and customer service representatives occur from using offshore outsourcing groups.

Business outsourcing can save your company a lot of money. However, it is for you to decide which is more important, your customer satisfaction with your customer service and support or the amount of money you are saving through your outsourcing endeavors.

You may find your customer count goes down once you begin outsourcing your customer service needs.

Chapter 3: Selecting the Right Person

When you select your outsourcing professional from a freelance job site, there are several ways in which you can make sure you are selecting the right person.

Firstly, you have to ensure that you make all the project details quite clear. Write about everything you expect. These are the things your project post should cover.

- The nature of your work.
- The amount of work in total.
- Any milestones, like if you want the work to be completed in small chunks and within what frame of time.
- The time you can give for the completion of the whole project.
- The price you are willing to pay.
- Any special qualifications you are looking for in your employees.
- Any characteristics that you don't want in your employees.
- Special points that you will need to make your decision, such as samples.

Most importantly, make sure that you post the project in the right category. People will get alerts only based on the categories they have applied for. So, if you put your project in the wrong category, the right people aren't going to get it.

When you take care to spell out as many details as you can, you can be almost sure that you will get the right people bidding on your work. You may get a few bids, but they will be quality bids.

Make sure to check out all the samples of their work, because this is your most important judging point. If you want an original sample, you can mention that in your project post itself, and people who are willing to give you an original sample of their work will do so.

In any case, it is a good idea to only post a short-term project initially till you build a trust factor with an employee. Once that is set up, you can go for longer-term projects.

Choose people for the following qualifications:

- The quality of their work, which you can see through their samples.
- The ratings and reviews they have obtained on the site.
- Their responsiveness – It is very important they respond to your emails quickly and it is best if they have an instant messaging id that they can use.
- Their pricing – Price shouldn't be an important factor unless you are working on a budget.

Once you get a good professional, make sure you pay them promptly and give them a review according to their work. This ensures they will stay with you long and you won't have to undergo the hassle of looking for employees repeatedly.

Business Outsourcing And Verifying Employees

When you decide upon business outsourcing for project needs it is important to verify who the people are who will be working in your business. You should verify the employees as you would your own.

If you run background tests on your employees, then you should do the same with an outsourcing business's employees.

It will be hard for you to demand that outsourcing employees agree to a background check or a drug test.

What you can do is use only a company that will provide proof to you the people are acceptable. You should get the name of every person who will be entering your business working on the project.

Sometimes when there are a lot of people entering the business from an outsourced company it can be confusing who is with the company and who is in the building without authorization.

Be sure you know each employee who works for the outsourced company and provides them with temporary badges to wear. This way, anyone who is not wearing one of the temporary badges can be questioned with reason.

Your employees have a right to feel safe at their place of work. You cannot bring in people who have dangerous backgrounds to work on an outsourced project for you.

You should verify all of the provided information and know every person who will be working on an outsourced project. All of these employees from the business outsourcing company should be properly introduced to your staff so everyone feels comfortable with the people walking through the halls.

Chapter 4: Outsourcing Professionals from Online Jobsites

Since online job sites are the best places for you to get professionals, let us look at them in a little more detail.

Here are some of the advantages of getting professionals from here:

- People you will find on the job sites have registered here with the express intention of finding work. Many job sites are free to join, but some require paid memberships. Being a paid member may reflect a bit more on their sincerity about being professional. Hence, you can be sure you get some sincere people to give your work to.

- There are various ways in which you can find how good a particular worker is. Every job site has a rating and review system (for the employee as well as the employer). This helps you decide.

- All websites have an escrow system. This takes care of all disputes. Once an escrow is made, the website will arbitrate any problems that arise.

- You can make detailed project posts, outlining clearly what you want to be done, what time and budget you can afford. People make bids accordingly, so you can be sure you won't have to bargain.

- You can ask people to show samples of their past work.

- You can also invite people to bid on your project.

It is very simple to post projects on online job sites. Many of them, allow you to post projects for free. You only have to post all details of the work as you want it, spell out the timeframe and the budget you can offer, and post it in the relevant category.

Once your project is live, which is instantaneous, people start bidding. Then, all you have to do is to look at the bids closely and make your decision on whom to select for your job.

You cannot communicate personally with the bidders till you select them. However, there is a private message board that helps you communicate with them, subject to certain restrictions (like you cannot give out your personal contact details in any way). This helps you decide better about whom to select.

Many people are forging fruitful and long-term work relationships through these online freelance job sites, irrespective of geographical barriers, and getting mutually benefited.

Without the hassle of actually needing employers on their premises, they can get their work done professionally and, in most cases, in cheaper ways as well.

Maintaining Quality of Service When Business Outsourcing

When you have poorly defined your contract with a business outsourcing company, the quality of the project may suffer severely.

There are many things you can do to verify the project maintains the expected quality when you are using a company other than yours.

When you define the objectives for the project you want to be completed, they need to be defined clearly and everyone needs to acknowledge and sign off that they agree to them. You should not forget anything.

Being too picky is better than not being specific enough. By forgetting certain things and not specifying them you are opening a door for poor work to be done.

When this happens, you cannot request it be changed and done a different way because it was not specified in the contract.

What will happen, is that you will have to pay additional money to have things done the way you want because you didn't properly specify in the contract.

One person should not write the specifications for the project. Projects need to be written by everyone who will be involved and affected by the project.

You need to be sure you don't miss anything that might cause poor quality with the project. If you need to research equipment and how things are properly done, then you should. Many people can be affected by poor quality in a project such as your employees who are using the equipment.

However, shareholders and stakeholders also have a vested interest that the money being spent on an outsourced project is spent well.

You don't want to be out of a job because you were not clear about how the project needed to be done and now you have a completed project, but it makes your customers very unhappy.

Chapter 5:

Understanding

Outsourcing

Outsourcing is a term that has received a great deal of attention lately.

Despite the increasing trend in companies relying on outsourcing, there are still some who do not clearly understand what is meant by the term outsourcing.

This chapter will examine some of the key elements of outsourcing to help the reader develop a better understanding of the concept of outsourcing.

Outsourcing Defined

What is outsourcing? This is the most basic question many have about the subject of the outsourcing. They are not yet interested in more complex aspects of the issue because they have not yet grasped the most basic understanding of the process. In the simplest language outsourcing is when a company delegates the completion of certain tasks to an individual not employed by the company directly. This individual may be an independent contractor or an employee of another company who is subcontracted to complete these tasks. In exchange for the individual's services, he or his company receives monetary compensation.

This description of outsourcing makes it far easier to understand the concept. Most people incorrectly assume outsourcing only applies to situations where large corporations have products manufactured overseas by a subsidiary and don't realize examples of outsourcing can be seen just about everywhere in corporate America.

Domestic Outsourcing

Domestic outsourcing refers to outsourcing where both the primary company and the independent contractor or subsidiary are located in the same country. One of the main reasons for outsourcing is to reduce costs but it is not always necessary to outsource work overseas to reduce costs.

Cost savings will be discussed in greater detail in the section on the benefits of outsourcing but essentially outsourcing results in savings as a result of a reduction of labor costs.

Overseas Outsourcing

Overseas outsourcing is the type of outsourcing most people already understand. This is where large corporations such as Nike, and even some smaller companies, employ manufacturing plants overseas in third world countries to upsize their profits.

This is significant because their costs including wages, materials, and building lease would be considerably higher in the United States than they are in these other countries.

Benefits of Outsourcing

Now that you have a clearer understanding of the concept of outsourcing, you might wonder why companies would go to the trouble of outsourcing certain tasks. Outsourcing is popular because there is a lot of benefits to the companies who outsource the work.

Some of the benefits include:

- Reduced labor costs
- Increased workforce
- Greater flexibility

One of the main reasons companies resort to outsourcing is it can significantly reduce costs. In the case of overseas outsourcing of manufacturing tasks, costs can be cut dramatically because there are lower wages and costs associated with managing and maintaining the manufacturing plants.

However, companies also enjoy cost savings when they outsource tasks domestically. Reduction of labor costs is the primary source of savings in this case. Independent contractors hired on a contract basis for the purpose of completing specific tasks are often not given benefits such as social security, Medicare, and workers' compensation.

Another benefit of outsourcing is enjoying a larger workforce without actually hiring additional employees. Companies that maintain networking relationships with qualified individuals have more opportunities open to them because they are able to rely on these individuals to assist them if they acquire large or complicated projects.

Finally, outsourcing gives a company a great deal of flexibility. Companies that have a significant workload and backlog of work where the majority of the employees are highly utilized might be hesitant to compete for new work because they do not have a great deal of employee availability.

However, with a network of individuals to rely on if they need to outsource arises, the company has more flexibility in pursuing new work.

The Advantages of Outsourcing

Outsourcing has become a very popular alternative for a number of very valid reasons. Outsourcing initially emerged as a way for companies to cut costs by having processes such as manufacturing and assembly done in overseas locations where costs were much lower. Lower wages and operating costs both contributed to these reduced costs.

These lower costs were appealing because they greatly improved the profit margins for the companies. However, outsourcing is now gaining in popularity for a variety of other reasons.

While cost reduction is still a primary advantage, other elements such as access to industry experts, a larger workforce, and more flexible options are being embraced as welcomed advantages offered by outsourcing.

Cost Reductions From Outsourcing

As previously mentioned, reducing costs was the original purpose of outsourcing and although outsourcing has since been demonstrated to have other significant advantages, cost reduction still remains one of the prime advantages.

Companies look to outsource tasks that would be more costly to complete in-house. An example of this type of task would be a software-related task requiring specialized training. Companies that do not have an on-staff employee qualified to complete this task can benefit financially by outsourcing this task.

There may be significant fees required to retain the services of an industry expert on a contractual basis, but the efficiency of this individual will enable him to complete the task much more quickly than it could have been done in-house.

If the task were not outsourced an in-house employee would have had to complete the task and may have taken significantly longer costing the company more in the long run.

On-Call Experts

In the previous section, we discussed how having industry experts available to complete outsourced tasks can result in cost savings for the company but having these experts on call also provides the potential for new opportunities for the company. With experts waiting in the wings to assist, the company is able to go after larger and more specialized types of work. This is important because in doing this the company can find themselves enjoying greater prosperity.

A Larger Workforce

Still another advantage to outsourcing is the benefit of enjoying a larger workforce when necessary without the hassle of maintaining a larger staff.

Through outsourcing companies can bring in additional employees on a contract basis during times of prosperity without worrying about having to lay them off or keep them utilized when the surge of work begins to wane. This is particularly relevant in industries that enjoy peak seasons as well as off-seasons.

Another advantage of having a larger workforce is the ability to generate a larger profit. This is important because smaller companies can find themselves in a position where they can compete with larger companies for bigger jobs by outsourcing a portion of the workload.

More Flexibility

Finally, more flexibility is another considerable advantage of outsourcing work. Even the most well-planned projects may suddenly end up behind schedule or under a time crunch due to minor errors, changes in plans, or other incidental activities.

Smaller companies who do not have the resources to compensate for these inevitable mishaps may find themselves in serious trouble without the ability to outsource work when necessary.

These companies can take advantage of outsourcing in times of trouble to help them deal with problems without alienating clients or performing poorly on a project.

Chapter 6: When Outsourcing Is the Best Solution

There are times when outsourcing is the only option available for reasons such as no in-house employees are qualified or available to complete the particular task.

However, there are also times when outsourcing is not the only option, but it is also the best option. In these situations, outsourcing becomes a wise business decision as opposed to a requirement or a matter of personal preference. This chapter will discuss three situations where outsourcing is the best option.

These options include:

- When outsourcing saves money.
- When outsourcing helps make deadlines.
- When outsourcing increases productivity.

When Outsourcing Saves Money

Outsourcing becomes the best solution when it saves the company money without compromising the quality of the work. Companies whose goals are predominately financial in nature often focus on the bottom line in determining whether or not to outsource projects or tasks.

When the cost savings result in inferior work it is certainly not the best solution. However, companies who are able to outsource projects to highly qualified and capable individuals while still saving money enjoy the benefit of knowing they selected the best solution for their software related problems.

Whether or not outsourcing saves money is a concept which many have difficulty understanding. When most people think of outsourcing, they picture citizens of third world countries working for substandard wages, but this is not an accurate representation of outsourcing.

Nowadays outsourcing often involves hiring high-priced, domestic consultants to tackle complex software problems under aggressive deadlines.

This explanation makes the issue even more confusing for some who think it is impossible for it to be less expensive to hire a high-priced consultant than to complete the task in-house.

Examining labor costs is often necessary to see how outsourcing can often reduce costs. Outsourcing may carry a higher per hour rate, but it is important to note that the company is often not required to pay benefits such as social security, Medicare, and workers' compensation to the consultant.

Additionally, the consultant may work offsite meaning he is not putting a drain on company resources. Examining these factors is necessary to determine whether or not outsourcing is the best option.

When Outsourcing Helps Make Deadlines

Aggressive deadlines often make outsourcing the best available option. Most companies do not want to have to turn down work because they do not have enough staff members available to complete a particular project.

Having the ability to outsource software jobs makes it easier for a company to compete for more jobs than their staff could possibly handle. This is because the management knows they have a network of consultants to rely on during times when schedules are tight. In these cases, outsourcing becomes the best option.

Whether schedules are originally set to be rather aggressive or become accelerated due to problems earlier in the project they can become a hassle for many companies. Regardless of the cause of the scheduling concerns, clients may not understand if the consultant is unable to meet the required deadlines.

When Outsourcing Increases Productivity

Outsourcing also becomes the best solution to a problem when it results in increased productivity. Consider the tasks you intend to outsource and determine the amount of time it would take for these tasks to be completed in-house.

Now consider the amount of time it would take to have these tasks completed through outsourcing. If the answer is outsourcing would be quicker, it is logical to go ahead and outsource these tasks. The reason for this is the consultant can be more efficient with the tasks.

When considering productivity, it is also important to note that employees who are handling multiple tasks often take longer to complete each individual task than they would to complete each of these same tasks if they were his only responsibility.

This is because employees who are multi-tasking are not necessarily as efficient as they believe they are. The main problem with multi-tasking is when switching from one activity there is a small delay each time the employee switches tasks because he often has to review his recent progress and remind himself what he intended to do next.

Conversely outsourcing singular tasks allows the individual to focus 100% on each task.

When Outsourcing Is the Only Option

Deciding whether or not to outsource particular tasks is one of the many important decisions both large and small companies alike have to make often. This can be a difficult decision at times but often the decision-making process is greatly simplified, and it becomes clear that outsourcing is the only viable option.

Situations in which this may occur are when the in-house staff is not qualified for these tasks when the in-house staff is already overburdened and when specific client requirements are specifying certain tasks must be completed by individuals with specific qualifications.

This part of the chapter will address each of these situations and discuss why outsourcing becomes the only solution in each case.

The Qualification Of In-House Staff

Sometimes outsourcing becomes the only option available because there are no in-house staff members qualified to perform a particular task. This often occurs when a task requires a highly specialized degree or area of expertise.

This is especially problematic when the task in question is an extremely rare one. When this is the case it does not make sense for a company to hire an employee with these capabilities when they will be rarely utilized because employees who are not productive are expensive to the company.

However, if this task becomes one that is required regularly, the question of whether or not to outsource the task becomes more complicated. As this part of this chapter is focusing on situations where outsourcing is the only option, we will not delve further into the factors which complicated this decision such as labor costs and increased manpower.

Smaller companies often face the problem of not having staff members qualified for particular tasks more often than larger companies. Larger companies obviously have a larger pool of employees to pull from and it is therefore much more likely for the smaller firms to have gaps in their level of expertise than it is for larger companies to have these gaps.

The Availability Of In-House Staff

Sometimes outsourcing becomes the only option based on staff availability. A company may have a need for tasks to be completed rather quickly. Although it may be a task for which several in-house employees are qualified, current workloads may make it impossible for these employees to take on these tasks.

When this occurs, outsourcing again becomes the only option. Company employees are often multi-tasking and may be working towards several serious deadlines at any one particular time.

Management is tasked with the responsibility of doling out work to lower-level employees and when they feel as though their in-house staff is not able to take on more work, they often turn to outsource as a solution.

Workloads often become a factor in outsourcing when there are projects which are particularly time-sensitive in nature. Employees and employers often have to prioritize the multiple tasks they are managing but there are times when a number of projects or tasks become urgent simultaneously and when this happens it may become difficult to complete all of these tasks with only the assistance of the in-house staff.

Client Requirements

Sometimes outsourcing becomes the only option as a result of client requirements. Depending on the complexity of a task, a client may require the consultant firm tasked with completing a task to have the task performed by an individual with specific qualifications.

These qualifications may include specific training in certain types of software, exact education requirements, or previous work experiences. Companies that do not have in-house employees who meet these specific requirements have no choice but to outsource the task to a qualified individual.

When this is an isolated incident, companies often outsource the task and do not make efforts to attempt to hire a full-time employee with these qualifications.

This is a wise decision especially when the client requirements require an expert in a particular niche of the software industry. Employing an employee of this caliber would likely be rather expensive especially if he would rarely be called upon to utilize his advanced skills.

Chapter 7: Internet Marketing and Outsourcing

Internet marketing and outsourcing work very well together. In fact, most Internet marketers employ to lease some degree of outsourcing.

The most common aspects of Internet marketing that are outsourced are copywriting and website design. Ideally, these tasks will be delegated to individuals who are skilled in search engine optimization (SEO).

Additionally, those who manage multiple niches may opt to outsource the responsibilities of managing some of their niche markets. This chapter will take a look at some of the commonly outsourced tasks and provide information regarding why outsourcing these tasks are ideal.

Managing Multiple Niches

Many involved in Internet niche marketing become involved in managing multiple niche marketing campaigns. When this happens, it can become difficult for one individual to oversee all of the campaigns without compromising the quality of the niche markets.

Therefore, he will often outsource the oversight responsibilities related to managing some of the niche markets. This gives him the freedom to focus more on developing new niches and marketing strategies as opposed to overseeing minute details.

Care should be taken when outsourcing this type of work to ensure the employee hired to undertake these tasks is an honest individual with a great deal of integrity.

Those who are lacking in integrity may take advantage of this situation to learn about the marketing strategies for the express purpose of stealing sensitive information and creating competition in these niches.

Outsourcing Copywriting

Copywriting services are also commonly outsourced in niche marketing. Those involved in Internet niche marketing realize the importance of providing high-quality content that is also optimized for search engines. This applies to copywriting, which is included on niche websites, in e-newsletters, in press releases, and in eBooks.

The content provided is critical to the success of the niche marketing campaign because it is often the first impression members of the target audience get off the campaign. Their opinion of the copy can determine whether or not they are willing to visit the niche website in the future or further research products or services for sale.

When selecting a writer to provide the content for the niche marketing campaign, it is important to consider a writer with SEO experience. This is important because the content provided on websites can have an impact on the search engine rankings of the website. The use of keywords is the most important part of copywriting relevant to SEO. The keywords should be used in a manner that creates an informative and interesting copy that appeals to both website visitors and search engines.

Outsourcing Website Design

Web design is another aspect of Internet niche marketing that is often outsourced. Most marketers recognize website design as an important part of their success.

They need their websites to be well designed both aesthetically and technically to ensure visitors enjoy the website and all of the features of the website operate smoothly.

Additionally, it is very important for the website designer chosen to understand how to implement SEO strategies into the design of the website.

There are many different strategies available for SEO and there are also always new techniques being developed, tested, and evaluated. The SEO of a website is pretty much a full-time job. This is why marketers need to outsource this work so they can ensure they have someone working on their website optimization constantly.

When Outsourcing Compromises Quality

The simple answer to this question is yes, and no and maybe. Well, maybe it is not such a simple answer because it is a particularly loaded question.

The subject of outsourcing is a very sensitive issue for many. There are some who believe that outsourcing, whether it is overseas or domestic, is taking jobs away from qualified individuals while others who are profiting from outsourcing are firm advocates for the practice.

In this section of this chapter, we will take a look at outsourcing and will examine scenarios when quality is compromised as well as scenarios when quality is not compromised.

What Is Outsourcing?

For those who are confused about what outsourcing entails, this section will explain the issue. In its most basic form, outsourcing is employing an individual outside of the work organization to perform specific tasks for monetary compensation. Outsourcing can be done on a per-project basis, for a set period of time, or on an ongoing basis for an undetermined period of time.

For many, the word outsourcing has a very negative connotation. When they think of outsourcing, they picture underage employees in third world countries working for salaries that would be paltry by our standards. However, outsourcing has evolved so much and no longer resembles this stereotype.

In fact, many outsourcings take place domestically by savvy entrepreneurs who market their abilities as an independent contractor rather than toiling away in corporate America. These individuals, enjoy their quality of life, negotiate fair compensation for their work, and accept or decline work at their own will.

Furthermore, these individuals are often highly qualified for the positions they accept and are capable of producing work of a high standard.

Do You Compromise Quality With Outsourcing?

The simplest answer to this question is quality is compromised when price becomes the sole governing factor in selecting a candidate to complete the outsourced task.

Of course, this answer is not completely accurate because the truth is there are very educated and skilled employees overseas who are fully capable of completing tasks just as well as those living in this country and often for a much lower price. However, when only domestic candidates are being considered and the price is the governing factor, quality is often compromised as it is very rare that the most qualified candidate is also the candidate with the lowest rates.

However, it is very common for an individual or a business to allow price to become more important than the quality of work. When this happens, quality is often compromised for the sake of a larger profit.

An example of this is seen regularly on websites where outsourcing projects are listed, and potential applicants submit their bids for these projects. Many who utilize these websites routinely select the lowest bidder without regard for the qualifications of the bidder. In most cases these individuals find they make a costly mistake when the work they receive is inadequate.

When Outsourcing Does Not Compromise Quality?

Outsourcing does not always compromise quality. In fact, in many cases outsourcing is not only the most affordable option but also provides the most qualified candidates. One way to avoid the pitfalls of having quality compromised by outsourcing is to carefully screen candidates before making a decision.

This process should be taken just as seriously as hiring a full-time employee because the work of the individual will reflect on you as an individual or your business. If due diligence is given to selecting the right candidate, it is not likely that quality will be compromised.

When outsourcing work to an individual it is important to request detailed information regarding their qualifications and to verify all information supplied.

Examples of information to request include:

- Previous work history
- Relevant work experiences
- Explanation of qualifications

Additionally, it is wise to ask for both business and personal references. These references should all be contacted and questioned about the work ethic and personal integrity of the individual.

Outsourced Not Outsmarted

There are many who tout the advantages of outsourcing as essentially a little-known secret to success. There are certainly a number of distinct advantages to the process of outsourcing.

Some of the most notable advantages include cost reductions, increased possibility for-profit, and the existence of a larger workforce without maintaining a staff of salaried employees.

All of these incredible advantages may make outsourcing seem as though it is an ideal resource in all situations, but this is not true. Certain precautions should be taken when outsourcing a project. It is important to be mindful of these precautions when outsourcing a project to ensure the project runs smoothly.

Verify Candidate Qualifications

When outsourcing a task or project to an individual, care should be taken to screen all applicants carefully before deciding to outsource the work. This is important because you want to be sure to outsource the work to a qualified individual.

Awarding a project to an unqualified individual can be a costly mistake if they turn in subpar work at the conclusion of the project. It can also be costly if it results in unnecessary delays or setbacks as a result of the lack of qualifications.

One way to avoid being outsmarted by fancy resumes hyping the accomplishments of an individual is to verify all of the information on the resume before awarding the project. This may entail contacting previous employers as well as references to determine the capabilities and work ethic of the individual. Taking the time to verify the information on the resume can help to ensure the individual you outsource the work to is truly qualified to complete the project.

Outline Project Requirements Carefully

When outsourcing a project, it is important to be very clear in outlining the project requirements. This is important so both the client and the independent contractor understand all of the requirements of the outsourced project.

Preparing contract documents stating the exact project details and compensation to be provided is a good idea as well. Taking this extra precaution will ensure the client does not have to pay fees until the contract specifications are met. A contract can also be helpful if disputes arise and mediation is required to resolve the conflicts.

Additionally, it is wise to include information regarding the required deliverables in the contract documents. This should include the exact end product which should be submitted.

In this portion of the document, the client can specify information regarding whether they require the project submitted as a hard copy of the completed project, a soft copy of the completed project, or both.

Schedule Periodic Milestone Meetings

Regularly scheduled progress status meetings are very important when a project is outsourced. These meetings should be scheduled often enough to ensure the project does not fall too far behind schedule during any one phase of the project. These meetings can be helpful to both the client and the independent contractor.

The client will benefit because they will remain in control of the project and can intervene if the independent contractor is heading in the wrong direction with the project. These meetings are also beneficial to the independent contractor because they can prevent him from being caught by surprise at the conclusion of the project if he misinterpreted the project requirements.

Chapter 8: Raising the Bar through Outsourcing

The stereotypes associated with outsourcing are often very negative in nature.

However, it is actually possible to utilize the concept of outsourcing to receive the highest quality of work possible. Outsourcing no longer only refers to overseas sweatshops where employees work long hours for meager pay.

Outsourcing now also occurs domestically and often at prices that are more than generous. Thanks to savvy entrepreneurs who realize the benefits of offering their services on a contract basis, outsourcing has become the wave of the future.

This chapter will take a look at how outsourcing can actually lead to superior work and increased profitability.

Top Quality Work from Industry Experts

One of the most advantageous aspects of outsourcing is the ability to employ industry experts for the completion of certain tasks. This becomes beneficial in situations where a business is faced with a complex problem that is beyond the expertise of the in-house employees.

Outsourcing gives the business the opportunity to outsource the task of solving the problem to a highly qualified candidate. Although the business may pay a hefty sum for the individual's services this fee will likely be significantly less than what it would have cost them to solve the problem with their in-house staff.

The amount of time it would have taken coupled with the potential for costly mistakes makes it clear outsourcing is the right decision in this scenario.

Another scenario where tasks may be outsourced to an industry expert is when the business is faced with the task of performing more work than they are capable of handling in-house.

During aggressive deadlines or unexpected delays, outsourcing can be used to complete projects according to unyielding deadlines.

Flexibility In Scheduling

Many businesses balance the workload they take on based on the number of employees they have on staff capable of assisting in each individual task. However, outsourcing gives businesses the ability to consider accepting more work than their in-house employees are capable of completing.

An example of when this is beneficial is when consultants are awarded more projects than they had anticipated and are suddenly in a situation where they are not able to meet their deadlines due to larger than anticipated workloads.

Another advantage of outsourcing is the ability to take on larger projects than usual. One of the most elementary factors often considered when awarding projects to consultants is the number of staff members who are available to work on the project.

Clients evaluate this number with their project needs and schedule to determine whether or not they think the consultant is capable of completing the project on time. Consultants who outsource portions of their projects are effectively able to increase the number of employees they can afford to have to work on a particular project.

Reduced Operating Costs

Finally, outsourcing can help companies to produce higher quality work by enabling them to reduce their operating costs. Outsourcing can save companies a great deal of money because they often do not have to pay benefits such as social security, workers' compensation, and Medicare to those who perform work on a contract basis.

Additionally, those who perform the outsourced work typically do the work from their own office meaning the company does not have to provide resources for the individual. Although these costs may seem trivial, they can really add up especially if outsourcing is used on a regular basis.

Combined with reduced operating costs, many companies find that productivity is increased through outsourcing. By outsourcing work to qualified individuals, the in-house employees are freed of additional responsibilities and can focus exclusively on the tasks they were hired to perform. This is significant because without outsourcing these same employees might be tasked with attempting to perform complicated tasks for which they are not properly trained or qualified.

When this happens there is a significant decline in productivity as the employees take longer than necessary to complete the more complicated tasks and do not have time to complete the simpler tasks.

Protect Your Niche When Outsourcing

In the world of Internet niche marketing, the greatest asset is often the chosen niche. Many marketers spend a great deal of time, energy, and resources selecting a niche that they believe is going to be profitable.

There are certainly no guarantees a particular niche will be profitable but there are certain strategies for choosing a niche that has a high probability of success.

One popular strategy for selecting a niche involves employing a principle similar to the concept of supply and demand. Statistical information supplied by search engines is used to determine the popularity of certain search terms.

This information is significant because terms that are being searched frequently are terms that have a large audience of Internet users looking for more information on the niche subject. These are terms that are in high demand.

From this statistical information, you can build a list of potential niches. Once this list is compiled, it is time to begin researching the competition in each of these niches. Ideally the niche you select will be one that has a large audience and not much competition. These are niches that are in low supply.

Choose The Type Of Work You Outsource Carefully

One way to protect your niche is to be selective about the type of work you outsource to others. Many Internet niche marketers are comfortable outsourcing their copywriting and their website design.

However, they are more protective about outsourcing tasks such as marketing, niche selection, and keyword development. This is because although copywriting and website design both involve optimization for keywords the strategies for doing so are readily available on the Internet. However, many marketers have specific methods for marketing and developing a niche and keywords and are not willing to outsource this work because it will likely involve sharing secret strategies.

Share Keywords via Email

Developing related keywords for the niche is a very important part of the success of an Internet niche marketing campaign. Keywords are absolutely critical and conventional wisdom holds that an extensive list of keywords should be developed for a particular niche to be successful. Some in the industry recommend developing approximately 200 keywords for each niche.

There is a great amount of effort put into the process of selecting keywords and those who are savvy do not want to make it possible for others to find their list of keywords on the Internet. Including a list of keywords on an advertisement seeking a copywriter or website designer will be searchable by others in the industry.

For this reason, it is not wise to post keyword lists where others have free access to the keywords. This may sound overly paranoid, but it is commonly known that Internet marketers often make the mistake of posting their keywords on job boards, and those who are interested in harvesting these keywords visit these websites frequently to gather information.

Transmitting the keywords through a protected email account or via telephone is a better way to protect the work you have put into developing your niche.

Use a Non-Disclosure Agreement

Finally, a non-disclosure agreement (NDA) is one way for the marketer to protect his niche when he is outsourcing. An NDA is essentially a document specifying the rights of the employer and employee in regard to sensitive materials. The NDA can be drafted to include any terms the client sees fit.

Some example of the restrictions the contractor may agree to by signing an NDA are:

- A definition of which materials are sensitive.
- Restrictions on how materials can be transmitted.
- A stipulation precluding the contractor from competing in the niche during a given time period.
- A duration of time for which the contract is binding.

In protecting a niche market, the above terms can be used when outsourcing. The client may specify the sensitive materials to be the niche and the related keywords as well as any information regarding marketing strategy.

The client may limit the methods in which sensitive materials can be transmitted to secure emails and telephone conversations. The duration of time for which the contract is binding is up to the client. Common timeframes include the duration of the project or a set number of days, weeks, months, or years.

In niche marketing, a timeframe of at least one year after the project is completed is recommended to prevent the contractors from entering the same niche immediately after the project ends.

Conclusion

If you are like most Internet marketers, you often find yourself wearing a variety of hats.

Those involved in the industry of Internet marketing are a hard-working breed by nature and are typically not afraid to roll up their sleeves and become involved in all aspects of their marketing campaign.

From brainstorming to develop a niche to designing aesthetically appealing and well-optimized websites and from writing scintillating website content and intriguing press releases to remaining active on industry message boards, Internet marketers do it all.

However, problems arise as individuals become more successful. Their niche markets begin to thrive and increase in number and completing all of these different tasks for several different niches is no longer feasible.

This is when it is important to know what aspects of outsourcing to other qualified individuals. This chapter will take a look at outsourcing both copywriting and website design.

Outsourcing these two elements to professionals enables the Internet marketer to retain control of crucial elements of the business such as creating new niches and promoting existing niches.

These two components are the most critical and by retaining absolute control of these elements and overseeing other elements it is not likely the quality of the niche markets will be compromised by outsourcing.

Leave The Copywriting To The Professionals

The copywriting required for an Internet niche marketing campaign is one of the first elements which should be outsourced. The content you provide on your websites, as well as in press releases, sales letters, and eBooks is likely the first impression potential clients get of your niche market.

Logically, it stands to reason that your copy should be well written, concise, informative accurate, persuasive, and search engine optimized. With so many requirements it is obvious this work should be completed by a professional copywriter.

The services of a quality copywriter, especially one skilled in search engine optimization (SEO), maybe a significant expense with many copywriters charging close to $1.00 per word for optimized content and over 30 cents per word for the content which is not optimized.

However, those in the industry of Internet niche marketing realize the value of quality copy for their websites and are willing to pay these fees because they know they will be more than compensated by the success of their niche markets.

Let The Experts Design And Optimize Your Website

We have already discussed how writers with SEO skills are a valuable commodity, but it is also important to note that website designers who possess SEO skills are critical to the success of Internet niche marketing campaigns. SEO is so important because high search engine rankings can drive a great deal of traffic to a niche website.

Internet users constantly rely on search engines to find them the most useful information for particular search terms and as a result, it is not likely these same users will visit websites buried on the third or fourth page of search results.

More realistically, they will visit the first couple of links in the search results and find the answers they are seeking. This is why it is so important for those in the industry of niche marketing to invest in SEO.

Keyword density is one component of SEO which is usually handled by the copywriter. However, many other SEO strategies can be incorporated into the design of a website to bolster rankings. Some of these strategies are careful selection of domain names and titles, use of META and ALT tags, and clean website design that contains an easy to navigate sitemap.

These are just a few of the most basic SEO strategies but techniques and strategies for SEO change regularly as search engines adjust their algorithms and industry professionals attempt new techniques to improve their rankings.

SEO is not a simple process and is basically a full-time job. For these reasons hiring a website design firm with SEO, capabilities are critical to the success of Internet niche markets.

BUSINESS OUTSOURCING

Lightning Source UK Ltd.
Milton Keynes UK
UKHW020629210121
377450UK00012B/1119